Original title:
The Canopy Cacophony

Copyright © 2025 Creative Arts Management OÜ
All rights reserved.

Author: Evelyn Hartman
ISBN HARDBACK: 978-1-80567-164-0
ISBN PAPERBACK: 978-1-80567-463-4

Whispers Among the Leaves

In the treetops where squirrels play,
A parrot squawks in a funny way.
A raccoon juggles acorns with flair,
While the owls hoot, pretending to care.

Crickets chirp in a rhythmic beat,
As frogs hop and dance on tiny feet.
The bees buzz loudly, stealing the show,
While butterflies twirl in a vibrant flow.

Symphony of Shadows

Beneath the boughs where shadows cling,
The chipmunks plan a grand spring fling.
With tiny hats and dapper vests,
They dance and twirl, forgetting their nests.

The wind whispers secrets, playful and light,
As the moon peeks out, ready to ignite.
Mice join in, with dry leaves as drums,
Creating a racket, oh how it hums!

Echoes in the Overhead

In the air above, a chattering crowd,
With squirrels and birds, they're feeling quite proud.
A crow tells jokes, with a beak so wide,
While the pigeons laugh, and nowhere to hide.

The sun winks down, with a golden ray,
As the shadow puppets have their play.
Raccoons with maracas join in with glee,
Beneath the canopy, what a sight to see!

Rustle of the Woodland Choir

The trees sway gently, a whimsical tune,
While mice compose music by the light of the moon.
A bear in a tuxed with a violin,
Plays notes so sour, you can't help but grin.

A bulging frog croaks out a bass,
As fireflies dance, lighting up the space.
With each rustle and giggle, the forest ignites,
In this woodland choir, oh what delights!

Songs Carried on the Autumn Air

Leaves twirl and tumble down,
Squirrels dance in a nutty crown.
A crow caws out a silly tune,
While raccoons plot by the light of the moon.

Footsteps crunch on the golden floor,
Chasing shadows behind each door.
Pumpkin pies with faces grinned,
As laughter bursts, the fun begins.

Chasing wind like a playful kite,
Kittens chasing bugs with sheer delight.
Playing tricks on the crisp cool air,
As golden sunshine hangs everywhere.

A breeze whispers tales of old,
Where magic lives, and jokes are bold.
The world becomes a stage of cheer,
With giggles echoing far and near.

Chime of the Observer's Veil

The wind chimes sing in merry sport,
While cats conspire in a comical court.
Flash of feathers, a duck in a tie,
Waddling proudly, oh my, oh my!

A bear attempts to wear a hat,
But ends up tangled, imagine that!
Silly shadows leap and prance,
As squirrels take part in a nutty dance.

With giggles echoing through the trees,
Frogs play jazz, while bees buzz with ease.
A pumpkin laughs, "Oh you aren't sly,"
With each hilarious moment, we fly high.

Every rustle brings a laugh anew,
Nature chuckles in a funny hue.
Beneath the sky, where whimsy's real,
We're all just puppets in a playful reel.

Serenade of Swaying Sprigs

In the breeze, the branches bounce,
Squirrels dance, and acorns trounce.
Frogs croak jokes on lily pads,
While chatty birds make all the fads.

Leaves are laughing, rustling loud,
Bumblebees buzz, they feel so proud.
A squirrel slips, a nut takes flight,
And owls hoot jokes in the night.

The Melody of Migration

Geese in line, honking their tune,
Swapping tales beneath the moon.
Wings flap wildly, birds take flight,
Chirping laughter, what a sight!

Crickets strum their evening song,
While fireflies twirl all night long.
A lazy bat joins in the cheer,
As insects giggle, oh so near.

Lively Conversations in the Green

Beneath the trees, the critters chat,
A wise old turtle dons his hat.
Mice gossip 'bout their cheese-filled dreams,
While ants scheme up their clever themes.

The grasshoppers leap with glee,
Holding court with a bumblebee.
They trade tall tales of things they've seen,
In this lively, leafy scene.

Notes from the Nectar Seekers

Buzzing bees with bright berets,
Plot their course for sweet bouquets.
With sticky feet, they fill their sacks,
As butterflies join for sweet high jinx.

Hummingbirds hover, sip with flair,
While dragonflies dance in the air.
A flower yawns, and petals sway,
As gossip blooms throughout the day.

Murmurs Among the Branches

Squirrels chitter, plotting a heist,
Acorns tumble, oh, what a feast!
Birds gossip about a cheeky thief,
As leaves dance, mocking belief.

A raccoon wears a hat made of twigs,
He proudly swaggers, the king of digs.
While crickets hum in a jazzy spree,
Nature's show is free, you see!

Melodies Under the Green Veil

Frogs croak out a symphony loud,
While moths gather, forming a crowd.
A turtle joins with a slow, wise tune,
As shadows giggle beneath the moon.

Grasshoppers leap to a bouncy beat,
While bees buzz dance in a zigzag feat.
With every chirp, the trees join in,
Nature's antics could make you grin!

Treetop Reverberations

The wind whispers secrets to the pines,
While owls hoot, drawing funny lines.
A fox cracks jokes that make leaves shake,
While ants throw a party, for goodness' sake!

A parrot squawks, "Who's the best dressed?"
As squirrels debate who's truly blessed.
The forest echoes with laughter and cheer,
Each sound reminding us life's quite dear!

Nature's Choral Assembly

In the woods, all creatures convene,
For a concert that's fit for a queen.
A bat strums strings with a squeaky sound,
While hedgehogs tap dance upon the ground.

Elks provide rhythm with thumps and claps,
While turtles nod to the tuneful laps.
The symphony swells, a delightful spree,
Unity in humor is the key!

Vibrations of Verdant Spaces

Leaves are laughing, swaying about,
Branches dancing, wiggle and shout.
Squirrels juggling acorns with glee,
In this green show, come join the spree!

Bees buzzing secrets, a comic buzz,
Tickled by breezes, it's just because.
Flowers prance, in bright-colored halls,
Nature's sitcom, filled with loud calls!

Frogs croak jokes from their lily pads,
Whispered punchlines make us all glad.
Dancing shadows on the forest floor,
Who knew nature could offer so much more?

The sun's a spotlight, bright and bold,
As critters perform tales to be told.
Each leaf a program in this grand show,
With laughter echoing, everywhere we go!

Secret Chants of the Trees

Old oaks gossip, a rustling breeze,
Telling tales through the swaying leaves.
Nutty whispers from the branches flow,
As wise roots chuckle down below.

Caterpillars drumming on petals' skin,
While cheeky squirrels plot grand din.
Parrots squawking jokes, oh what a riot,
In this leafy mix, who needs a diet?

Hummingbirds zip, doing acrobats,
Tickling blossoms, like playful cats.
The thud of fruit makes a silly sound,
While giggles rise from the soft, rich ground.

In the forest's heart, laughter is shared,
Every critter knows they're well-prepared.
Nature's choir, in humor divine,
Sings its sweet song, so wonderfully fine!

Nature's Whispered Ballad

In the thickets, secrets are spun,
A melody played, oh what fun!
Frogs sing baritone, soft and deep,
While crickets hum, missing their sleep.

Fluttering wings, a raucous cheer,
Butterflies dance, spreading good cheer.
The rustling grass joins the tune,
Under the watchful eye of the moon.

Chirping birds with a comic flair,
Flipping through branches without a care.
The laughter of streams, bubbling bright,
Makes even shadows join in the light.

So gather 'round, where the wild things play,
Join the song in this quirky way.
Nature composes a funny refrain,
With each rustle and whisper, it's never plain!

Celestial Chorus of the Canopy

Stars wink above, in a giggling spree,
While owls deliver wisecracks with glee.
Moonlight dances on branches so high,
As clouds drift by, with a soft, sweet sigh.

In the night, a symphony plays,
Crickets and frogs join in the praise.
A canopy filled with shimmering dreams,
Where laughter drips down like rippling streams.

Fireflies twinkle, like disco lights,
Beaming and bobbing through magical nights.
Nature's nightclub, where all are invited,
For a funny party, everyone's excited!

So laugh with the stars, let your worries slip,
In this vibrant world, take a joyful trip.
The chorus of nature, so playful and bright,
Sings a hilarious tune under the night!

Twilight Tones of the Forest Canopy

In twilight's glow, the critters sing,
A squirrel twirls, it lost its spring.
The owls hoot loud, with slurred delight,
As fireflies dance, an odd ballet at night.

Beneath the branches, shadows play,
A raccoon rumbles, just lost his way.
The bushes rustle, what could it be?
A hedgehog rolling, oh what a spree!

With chirps and squeaks, the laughter spreads,
A pair of frogs jump, then fall on their heads.
The grasshoppers join, in crazy leaps,
While nature giggles as twilight creeps.

Their melodies rise like bubbles in air,
A cacophony of joy, beyond compare.
In this merry realm of leafy embrace,
The forest's quirks put smiles on each face.

Songs of the Hidden Heights

High above, the branches sway,
A parrot quips, come laugh and play!
The winds all whisper, tales of yore,
As monkeys chatter, what's in store?

A woodpecker drums a silly beat,
While raccoons shuffle, two left feet.
Bright butterflies flutter, wearing their best,
In this wild concert, they never rest.

The sun dips low, and giggles squeak,
An acorn drops, a nutty peak!
With mischief brewing in every nook,
Even a hedgehog steals a look!

So join the song from high above,
In the frolic and folly, there's plenty of love.
Laughter echoes through leafy halls,
As nature plays, and mischief calls.

The Wooded Chorus

In the heart of woods, a chorus calls,
With chipmunks jumping and bouncing off walls.
A beaver grins, a twig in his teeth,
As birds take turns, on branches beneath.

The deer, they prance, with tails held high,
While turtles ponder, oh me, oh my!
The ferns all shake, in rhythm divine,
As laughter bubbles like sparkling wine.

A rooster crows, with a wicked twist,
A hedgehog rolls, oh wait, he missed!
With every note, the forest sways,
In this joyful symphony, we dance and play.

From roots to tip, the tunes ascend,
Whimsy and cheer, around each bend.
In nature's heart, where silliness thrives,
The chorus of woods keeps laughter alive.

Serenading the Swaying Leaf

Up in the branches, a crooning song,
As crickets chirp, and the night grows long.
A leaf swings low, in breezy delight,
While a mouse tap-dances, igniting the night.

With shimmery glow, the moon takes a peek,
A badger rolls over, feeling quite sleek.
The splashes of laughter, like raindrops that fall,
As nature rejoices, it's fun for us all.

A squirrel spins tales, both tall and wide,
While owls wink softly, with nothing to hide.
Each twig that cracks brings giggles anew,
Under the canopy, laughter flows through.

In this wild waltz, we sway and grin,
With every rustle, a new friend jumps in.
So serenade softly, let laughter increase,
Amongst the leaves, there's joy and peace.

Chorus of the Canopied Chorus

In the treetops, squirrels dance,
Chasing shadows, take a chance.
Leaves are clapping, roots are groovin',
Even the chipmunks are now movin'.

Frogs are croaking a silly tune,
Raccoon prancing, under the moon.
Bees are buzzing, butterflies twirl,
Nature's mischief in a whirl.

Branches swing like a wild band,
Every critter gives a hand.
Caterpillars making their way,
To join the feast of a leafy buffet.

So clap your hands and stomp your feet,
Join the laughter, feel the beat.
In this forest, joy's the aim,
Who knew that nature had such fame?

Soundtrack of the Shimmering Shadows

Under the boughs, the shadows play,
Dance of light throughout the day.
Glowing fireflies, winking bright,
Make a jest of the fading night.

Crickets chirp in offbeat rhyme,
Toadstools giggle, having a good time.
Wiggly worms, they twist and shout,
Caught in the groove, they dance about.

Mice in bowties, strut with flair,
Chasing giggles through the air.
With each hop, they're full of cheer,
Who said shadows have to fear?

Swinging branches, laughing leaves,
Giggling echoes weave through eves.
Nature's playlist, oh so fine,
A wacky concert, pure divine!

Orchestrated by Owls at Dawn

Under the stars, the owls confide,
In a symphony, they take pride.
With a hoot and a turn of their head,
They orchestrate the night instead.

Squirrels play the fiddle just right,
As raccoons tap dance in sheer delight.
Every sound is a note, a laugh,
Nature's concert, a quirky staff.

Morning breaks with a silly cheer,
Hooting owls now disappear.
Mice join in with a squeaky song,
As sunlight lingers, all day long.

They've mastered a tune that's quite absurd,
Even the worms have lightly stirred.
In this dawn of laughter and glee,
Owls ensure we're wild and free!

Melodies of the Misty Morn

The mist rolls in, a blanket wide,
Birds chirp softly, side by side.
In the air, a ticklish sound,
As frolicking creatures gather 'round.

Bumblebees hum their wacky beats,
While woodpeckers tap to the sweet treats.
Caterpillars sway, feeling bold,
Dancing like they're spun from gold.

Frogs leap high for a silly splash,
Next to the pond with a joyful crash.
Every ripple holds a grin,
Nature's laughter, where fun begins.

Morning giggles are loud and clear,
Every creature brings such cheer.
In this mist, we sing along,
To the melodies of life's wild song!

Echoes of the Emerald Dome

In the trees, the squirrels jest,
Hiding nuts, they think they're best.
Chirps and trills, a wild ballet,
As birds yell, 'Hey! It's our buffet!'

Frogs croak tunes, a slippery jam,
While crickets plot, 'Let's roast a ham!'
Dancing leaves with a swish and sway,
All join in, with no delay!

A woodpecker plays on a hollow drum,
While ants march in, then bounce with some.
Branches sway like a carnival ride,
Nature's laughter, it cannot hide.

So come, my friend, join this spree,
In the emerald dome, wild and free.
Echoes of joy in every sound,
Where fun and laughter can be found.

Chants of the Woodland Skies

Bumblebees buzz in a sweet refrain,
While butterflies flutter like they've gone insane.
A raccoon winks with a daring grin,
Saying, 'Join me, let the fun begin!'

Trees gossip as the wind sneezes loud,
Their leaves shimmy, drawing a crowd.
A squirrel spins tales of nuts gone wrong,
While owls hoot their late-night song.

The sky giggles with clouds so puffy,
Painting the blue a tad too stuffy.
In this world, whimsy reigns supreme,
With laughter echoing, a daydream gleam.

So raise your voice, let the laughter rise,
In the woodland air, beneath playful skies.
Join the chants where silly hearts play,
In a dance of joy, we'll swing and sway.

Murmurs from the High Boughs

Chirpy chats from above the ground,
Where secrets of the trees abound.
A parrot cracks jokes with a wink,
While raccoons show off their acrobatic pink.

Mice in hats plan a soirée,
As the peacocks strut in a flamboyant display.
Each branch hums with giggles and cheers,
Murmurs of fun, erasing all fears.

Woodpeckers tap at a comic beat,
While rabbits hop, tapping their feet.
Laughter echoes through every lush layer,
As nature plays, the ultimate player.

So listen close to the rustling sound,
Life's silly moments truly astound.
In the high boughs where giggles resound,
Joyful whispers are always found.

Serenade of the Sunlit Glade

In the glade where sunlight winks,
Nature's choir laughs and blinks.
A frog leads the merry crew,
With a voice that squeaks a tune or two.

Butterflies tease with a swirl and twirl,
While hedgehogs do a little whirl.
Each rustle brings a chuckle and cheer,
As the magic of laughter draws near.

The sunbeams dance with a golden glow,
Tickling the grass, making it grow.
In this space where joy never fades,
Laughter weaves through sunlit glades.

So join the fun, let your spirit play,
In the serenade of this bright ballet.
Where every heart beats a lively tune,
Under the watchful eye of the moon.

Lullabies of the Lush Overhead

Bouncy squirrels play their tunes,
With nutty beats 'neath the silvery moons.
The frogs croak choruses with great delight,
As fireflies dance like stars in the night.

Raccoons tap-dance on tree branches wide,
While crickets orchestrate from the side.
A crazy symphony of nature's jest,
Not a single creature ever gets to rest.

Each leaf adds a note, a breezy flair,
Bumbling bees whirl like they just don't care.
In this theater of green, laughter's the key,
As chuckles emerge from the high-flying bee.

So grab your friends, take a merry seat,
For the forest show can't be beat!
In this wild concert where joy meets glee,
Let the lullabies sing you free!

Crescendo of the Cascading Branches

Branches sway, shimmy, and shake,
As the wind makes music, there's no mistake.
A chorus of leaves, a rustling spree,
That's one wild party up high in the tree!

Parrots squawk jokes that tickle the ear,
While frogs in tuxedos croon songs we can't hear.
Beneath their green gowns, the flowers do sway,
Twisting and twirling in a floral ballet.

Mice in the grass play their own mini tune,
Though it sounds more like raucous laughter at noon.
The giggles of critters, a whimsical sound,
In the concert of nature, hilarity's found!

So silliness reigns in this vibrant dome,
Where every critter feels right at home.
In this raucous affair of nature's bravado,
Let's hum along with the goofy bravado!

Nature's Melodic Tapestry

Winding vines spin tales up high,
As angry birds chirp, 'Oh me, oh my!'
Giggling streams let their laughter flow,
In a tangled web of nature's show.

Beetles march in a tick-tock parade,
With tiny hats and a charade,
While trees gossip in whispers of green,
Sharing secrets that they've seen.

The bouncy blooms wave, might fall at your feet,
As butterflies flutter to their own funky beat.
A squirrel juggles acorns, he's quite the sight,
His nutty antics a source of delight.

So grab your snacks, pull up a chair,
Join in the fun, and breathe in the air!
With nature's choir all singing in tune,
You'll leave this escapade over the moon!

Hushed Voices in the Underbrush

In the ferns, the whispers are silly and bright,
While ants play charades beneath the moonlight.
The grasshoppers pop like little green drums,
  Creating a rhythm 'til the owl hoots sums!

Ladybugs gossip, sharing their flair,
While beetles run races — though none seems to care.
A patch of daisies giggles with glee,
As butterflies tease, 'You can't catch me!'

Under a cloak of the starlit sky,
The laughter of critters floats gently by.
A raucous riddle wrapped in a hush,
In the heart of the wild, there's never a rush.

So listen closely to nature's soft laugh,
Join in the whimsy, don't let it pass!
For in every whisper, every soft call,
Lives the joy of the wild, and it's funny for all!

Harmonies of Hibernating Hearts

Bears in pajamas snore away,
While squirrels dance in a wild ballet.
Snowflakes tickle their sleepy toes,
As dreams of candy and honey flows.

Frogs croak tunes of a winter cheer,
While rabbits giggle, eating peas dear.
The moonlight shines with a wink and a grin,
As dreams of spring make everyone spin.

Reflections of the Rustling Treasures

Leaves rustle like laughter in the breeze,
Squirrels gossip with fantastic ease.
The acorns plot a great treasure hunt,
While raccoons sing songs that they front.

Branches sway like they've lost their minds,
When chipmunks bust out dance moves that bind.
The bushes chuckle in wiggly delight,
As nature plays tricks all through the night.

Sounds of Serenity in the Stillness

In the quiet, there's hoots and howls,
As owls wink slyly, performing their cowl.
Crickets chirp with laughter so bright,
While fireflies flicker as stars take flight.

Whispers of wind tickle the trees,
As the spider winks and turns to tease.
The night is alive with comical glee,
As critters conspire, just wait and see.

Echoing Euphoria from the Heights

Birds wear hats made of twigs and bold leaves,
As clouds play tricks, like mischievous thieves.
They tumble and roll in the brilliant blue,
While the sunlight giggles, "You can join too!"

Kites weave stories across the wide sky,
While breezes deliver a soft lullaby.
The mountains chuckle, their peaks holding high,
As nature's orchestra plays on the fly.

Layers of Life in the Canopy

In the trees, the squirrels prance,
Chasing tails in a wild dance.
Parrots squawk a silly tune,
While bees buzz like a cartoon.

High above, the branches sway,
As raccoons plot their grand play.
Frogs drop in with a loud splash,
Making all the laughter crash.

The leaves whisper jokes to the breeze,
As chipmunks scurry with such ease.
Caught in laughter, birds take flight,
Fluttering in hilarious delight.

Underneath the leafy green,
Life bursts forth, a lively scene.
From acorns tossed to playful brawl,
Nature's giggles echo for all.

Voices Above the Understory

A parakeet drops a cheesy line,
While monkeys dance, feeling fine.
An old owl tells tales at night,
His glasses slipping, what a sight!

Down below, the crickets chirp,
As turtles trade their slowest burp.
Grasshoppers leap with style and grace,
While snails join in the silly race.

The wind carries giggles up high,
Songs of laughter that never die.
Each branch holds secrets, bold and bright,
In this theater of pure delight.

Echoes tumble, tickle the air,
In this realm, there's joy to share.
With every rustle, a joke is spun,
Life is funny when it's all in fun.

Crescendo of Colors

Red leaves burst with vibrant flair,
As butterflies flit without a care.
The sun paints hues on every face,
Each color leads a silly race.

Frogs in costumes sing their part,
While ladybugs add to the art.
A chorus of chirps fills the sky,
As leaves giggle when breezes sigh.

All around, a vibrant blend,
Where laughter and colors never end.
In this lively painted scene,
It's a party like you've never seen!

With every twist, nature's spree,
A whimsical world, so carefree.
Join the giggles, dance and sway,
In a rainbow's light, let's play all day!

Odes of the Open Sky

Clouds drift in a playful chase,
As birds hold races in open space.
With a splash, a raindrop falls,
Tickling leaves in nature's halls.

The sun throws colors, bright and loud,
As shadows dance beneath the cloud.
Silly giggles roll in the breeze,
While ants form marching jokes with ease.

In the twilight, crickets hum,
Amidst the laughter, here they come.
A comet streaks with a wink and a grin,
As stars twinkle, inviting us in.

Here's to the skies, the wild delight,
Where every moment feels just right.
With joy in our hearts, let's lift our eyes,
In this world of fun that never lies.

Ballad of Bursting Buds

In a garden where giggles flow,
Bursts of color begin to glow.
Petals dance in a breezy swirl,
Not a care in the world, oh girl!

Buds bounce high on a trampoline,
Laughing at shadows—oh, what a scene!
Bees wearing hats pollinate with glee,
Caterpillars join, all wild and free.

Sunshine tickles the trees so bright,
Worms pretend they're in an acrobat fight.
Every flower has a joke to share,
While the daisies braid each other's hair.

With a splash of colors spry and bold,
These little beings, a joy to behold.
Nature's chuckles weave a funny tale,
Where every bloom laughs without fail.

Nocturne of the Nightingale's Nest

In a cozy nook where night birds croon,
A nightingale's laughter fills the moon.
Wings that twirl like ribbons of light,
Singing silly songs with delight.

Bugs throw a party, all dressed in style,
Fireflies blink and flash with a smile.
Crickets play hide and seek with the dew,
While owls roll their eyes at the hullabaloo.

With every note, the branches sway,
Nightingale giggles echo and play.
Stars wink at the silly scene below,
Nature's opera steals the show.

As the night unfolds its velvet cape,
Every critter dons a funny shape.
Amidst the shadows, laughter extends,
Nature knows how to make amends.

Whispers of Wisdom in the Wilderness

In the woods where the wise trees sigh,
Squirrels craft secrets that float on high.
Chatter flows like a bubbling brook,
Even the boulders are in on the hook.

The wise old owl spins yarns of delight,
While rabbits debate the best carrot bite.
Leaves rustle with laughter, a gentle shush,
Nature's council in a soft, leafy hush.

Laughter ripples through the trees so tall,
A chorus of fables, wisdom for all.
From bottom to top, every creature hears,
The giggles that flow like the coolest cheers.

With a tickle from branches, roots find their way,
Nature's humor brightens the day.
In every whisper, a chuckle blends,
The wilderness laughs, as joy transcends.

Threads of Life Among the Limbs

In a tapestry of twirling vines,
Laughter weaves through the swaying pines.
Branches shake, a funny dance ensues,
Even the squirrels giggle in twos.

As butterflies waltz and leaves swirl around,
Ants in tuxedos march proud on the ground.
Each laughter echoes, a playful hum,
Till the echo of joy makes the trees numb.

Vines whisper tales of grandeur and glee,
Of a picnic gone wrong, filled with spilled tea.
Feathers fly as the antics unfold,
With stories of silliness thoroughly told.

In this lively place with limbs far and wide,
Nature stands tall, full of comic pride.
Through the threads of life, laughter flows fast,
In the heart of the forest, fun is amassed.

Strains of Sunbeams Filtering Down

The sunbeams dance with glee,
Tickling leaves up high,
They whisper jokes to the trees,
As shadows start to fly.

A squirrel cracks a nutty pun,
While birds share comic tales,
The laughter echoes, oh what fun,
As sunlight paints the trails.

Frogs croak in ribbits so absurd,
While butterflies flutter with flair,
Each ray becomes a comic word,
That fills the fragrant air.

A breeze joins in the jesting spree,
Rustling leaves in playful chase,
Nature's laughter flows so free,
In this sunny, silly space.

Artistry Amidst the Arched Canopy

Beneath the arch of leafy art,
Brush strokes of laughter sway,
Crafted by nature's playful heart,
Compositions on display.

Crickets strum their silly strings,
While woodpeckers drum on high,
Each critter flaunts its silly bling,
As giggles float on by.

A rabbit poses with delight,
In a hat made of green grass,
As artist vines twist tight,
To join the laughter class.

This scenic joke, an open book,
Painted bright in vibrant hue,
Here all can share a comic look,
In nature's big debut.

Palettes of Peaceful Patter

Raindrops plop in cheerful tones,
Like a band of tiny drummers,
They mingle with the giddy groans,
Of squirrels plotting summers.

The ground is slick with nature's paint,
A canvas of muddy cheer,
Where toddlers splash, and laughter's faint,
While puddles draw them near.

Each droplet plays a funny role,
As frogs serenade the clouds,
In this quirky water bowl,
A stage for nature's crowds.

From branches high to gravel low,
The peaceful patter sparks delight,
A symphony in joyful flow,
As day turns into night.

Nature's Vibrant Annals Above

Among the leaves, the stories weave,
Of rhythm, rhyme, and jest,
With every rustle, tricks up sleeve,
Nature's humor is the best.

Clouds giggle, puffing round and bright,
Swinging by with silly grace,
They play hide-and-seek in flight,
In their ever-changing place.

A raccoon dons a scholar's cap,
Reciting tales from the ground,
While owls nod and take a nap,
To the laughter all around.

These tales rise high, a vibrant song,
Arching like a grand mural,
In nature's book where all belong,
The antics never mortal.

Rhythm of the Rustling Foliage

Leaves dance and flutter bright,
Squirrels bicker, what a sight!
Branches sway without a care,
Winds whisper secrets in the air.

Frogs croak in their silly tune,
Bugs tap dance beneath the moon.
Breezes laugh, they pull and tease,
Nature's madness, none can freeze!

Trees giggle in a gentle sway,
As sunbeams join the playful fray.
A jester crow, with feathers bold,
Tells tales of mischief, oh so old!

Join the laugh, it's quite the show,
In tangled greens where fun will grow.
With every rustle, every cheer,
A world of whimsy waits right here!

Harmony Among the Twisting Vines

Vines twirl and twist with flair,
Laughing ladybugs, what a pair!
Lizards leap with acrobats' grace,
In this wild, familiar place.

Bees buzz jokes as they amass,
Pollinating petals, oh what sass!
Roots play tag beneath the ground,
In their tangle, joy is found.

A snake in shades of vibrant green,
Sings a tune both bold and keen.
The party's wild, it's quite a scene,
While leafy hats sway in between.

Upside down, the world's a treat,
Twisting tales that can't be beat.
Within the vines, the mirth aligns,
Creating harmony that shines!

Songs of the Soaring Spirits

Birds belt out a chorus loud,
While squirrels scurry, feeling proud.
High above, the breezes play,
A raucous symphony today.

Clouds pass by in a soft embrace,
As butterflies join the race.
Winds whip round in a goofy swirl,
Creating chaos that makes us twirl!

With feathers bright, the joy they share,
As kites dance through the sunlit air.
A woodpecker's drum is quite the hit,
Knocking rhythms; it'll never quit!

In the heights where spirits sing,
Nature's winks, a playful thing.
So lift your heart, let laughter soar,
In a world where fun's in store!

Conversations with the Canopy Creatures

Chattering monkeys throw their jokes,
While porcupines crack up in pokes.
Turtles nod with a wise old grin,
As the laughter echoes; let's begin!

Fleeting shadows dance and glide,
Through treetops where giggles hide.
Chirpy critters share their plans,
Hosting tea with acorn fans.

Owls hoot with a wink so sly,
While raccoons plot as stars fly by.
In this gathering, whims reside,
Where every creature takes great pride!

From lofty branches, joys unfold,
In silly tales and friendship bold.
Join the chat, don't hesitate,
With canopy critters, fun awaits!

Dappled Light

In the quiet grove, they prance,
Lively leaves in a merry dance.
Each beam a spotlight, bright and spry,
Twirling shadows as squirrels fly.

Giggles echo through the air,
Sunbeams tangled in their hair.
Brightly colored, a sight to see,
Nature's jesters, wild and free.

With whispers low, they plot and scheme,
Picking acorns, a nutty dream.
Laughter lingers as they tease,
Each chirp a jig, each rustle a breeze.

Under branches, fun takes flight,
Sprightly antics, pure delight.
In the dappled, light they twirl,
Nature's tricksters, watch them whirl.

Unseen Voices

Hidden chatter fills the glade,
Mystery in the shade parade.
Whispers giggle, softly float,
Among the leaves, they sing and gloat.

Fluffy clouds, they nod and wink,
The trees have secrets, they all think.
Rustling leaves share silly tales,
Of high-flying squirrels and clever snails.

In the stillness, laughter breaks,
Filling gaps with playful quakes.
Every branch a gossip queen,
With stories wild, yet somewhat clean.

As owls chuckle, crickets hum,
Nature's choir knows how to drum.
Invisible voices, a joyful sound,
Echos of whimsy all around.

The Soundtrack of the Upper Realm

A raucous band among the leaves,
With chirps and clicks, their talent weaves.
Crickets strum their nightly tune,
While frogs croak under the moon.

A woodpecker drums a jaunty beat,
Squirrels whistle, oh so sweet.
The rustle of grass adds to the flair,
With every note, a wild affair.

In the thickets, laughter rings,
Singing birds with silly flings.
Harmony among the branches high,
Nature's party reaching the sky.

Tune in, tune out, swing along,
With every rustle, join the throng.
The upper realm plays a funny song,
An endless concert where all belong.

Storytellers of the Tallest Trees

With barky brows, the giants stand,
Telling tales across the land.
Great adventures, splendors old,
In their trunks, a magic bold.

Roots run deep with secrets shared,
Whispered stories, none are scared.
Branches sway as the yarns unfold,
Bolder than legends, brighter than gold.

Leaves lean in, all ears to hear,
Tales of mischief, cheer, and fear.
A raccoon's caper, a squirrel's shame,
Every old tree knows the game.

So gather near and listen close,
To the laughter of trees we love most.
In every whisper, a story gleams,
Of the forest, and all its dreams.

Lullabies Beneath the Lush

Beneath the canopy's leafy quilt,
Gentle whispers of dreams are built.
Crickets sing soft songs of night,
While fireflies flutter, lending light.

Babbling brooks weave sleepy tunes,
Morning glories whisper with the moon.
Each leaf a cradle, every breeze,
Lulling creatures to drift with ease.

Drowsy owls in a mellow state,
Chuckling softly, they find their fate.
Nature's music, a soothing balm,
In the lushness, everything's calm.

So rest your head where shadows fall,
Dream of capers with the nightfall.
In the cozy nook, let laughter spread,
With lullabies sung, sleep in your bed.

Rhapsody of the Bright Canopies

In branches thick with foliage bright,
A squirrel danced, quite out of sight.
He tripped on nuts and shared a grin,
As birds above burst out in din.

The sunbeams slipped through leafy spires,
While ants marched by, wearing tiny tires.
Each rustle made for playful cheers,
And laughter echoed through the years.

Dance of the Drifting Dewdrops

Dewdrops twirl in morning glow,
They leap and laugh, they put on shows.
A spider's thread becomes their stage,
As droplets spin with wild, bold rage.

The flowers chuckle in delight,
As petals join to dance in flight.
The breeze just giggles, can't resist,
While sunbeams wink and make a list.

Ballad of the Blossoming Boughs

Petals tumble like confetti fair,
A bee with swagger in the air.
He makes a joke, they all applaud,
With honey-laden laughs bestowed.

Branches shake with mirthful glee,
As new buds gossip joyfully.
The wobbly worms on branches sway,
In this tune of laughter, come what may.

Chorus of the Towering Trees

The trees are tall, but they all jest,
With little birds, they hold a fest.
A woodpecker knocks a silly beat,
While branches shake to rhythmic feet.

Leaves chatter softly, secrets shared,
Each gust of wind leaves them all scared.
Yet laughter lifts up through the blue,
In nature's concert, all feels new.

Révérence to the Rustle

In the woods, the leaves do dance,
Squirrels wear their best pants.
A twig snaps, the laughter grows,
As chipmunks debate the best circus shows.

The winds play tunes, quite a bit wild,
Even grumpy owls can't help but smiled.
A raccoon steals a peanut or two,
While rabbits argue over the best view.

Branches sway in a jovial spree,
Nature's giggles, oh so carefree.
Echoing jokers from every tree,
Whispering secrets of jubilee.

So let us bow to this rustling song,
In our hearts, where we belong.
With little critters and their cheeky plays,
We find delight in their quirky ways.

Tapestry of the Tall Trees

The trunks stand tall, taking a bow,
As squirrels debate, 'Who's king now?'
With branches weaving tales so bright,
A raccoon dons a hat, quite a sight!

The foliage flutters, a bright cartoon,
Songs of the forest, they sing at noon.
Whispers of laughter in every sway,
As the breeze invites us to join the play.

Wobbly woodpeckers knock on wood,
While butterflies giggle, oh, how they would!
A crow caws loudly, thinks it's a star,
While flowers chuckle, that's who we are!

In this tapestry, life's colors blend,
Nature's mischief seems never to end.
Let's dance with the shadows and light so free,
In this forest of giggles, you and me.

Pulse of the Pine Needles

In the pine grove, the needles sway,
They tickle the breeze, come out to play.
A porcupine sings with all its might,
While squirrels rehearsed for their big night.

Woodland critters hold a grand show,
With acorns as seats, all in a row.
Each performance, a laugh, a cheer,
Nature's comedy, oh so dear!

With a twist and a turn, the branches share,
Tales of mischief floating in the air.
And even the roots start tapping feet,
As puddles giggle at the funny beat.

The pulse of play from the trees above,
Nature's laughter, a treasure we love.
So join the feast and share the delight,
Stand tall, dear friend, let's dance through the night!

Luminous Legends of the Leaves

Leaves glow softly in the twilight,
Whispering tales of bravado and flight.
A leaf in a twirl brushes past my nose,
As frogs croak ballads in muddied prose.

Glowing fungi light the forest way,
As fireflies mimic stars in their play.
A hedgehog claps, the audience roars,
Nature's circus, with laughter galore!

Amidst the chirps, a joyful sound,
Branches shimmy, their spirits unbound.
With a wink from the moon, the night is fine,
As crickets swap stories over a pine.

In this luminous world, the fun won't cease,
With rustling leaves, we find our peace.
Join the revelry, shine bright, be bold,
For nature's annals are treasures untold.

Dances of the Dappled Sunlight

Fluttering leaves, a bright yellow tune,
Swaying in rhythm: what a silly boon!
Glimmers of laughter, twinkle and twist,
Each tree's a dancer, in the sunlight kissed.

Branches do cha-cha, with a jolly dip,
Squirrels join in, taking a wild trip!
The shadows all giggle, as they ripple and play,
Nature's own comedy, brightening the day.

Bees buzzing like drummers, they keep up the beat,
Flower petals waltzing, oh what a treat!
Ribbons of sunlight, a confetti parade,
In this joyous ballet, no feeling of shade.

So come take a gander, give a little whirl,
Join in the fun, give your laughter a twirl!
In this light-hearted frolic, leave worries aside,
In the sunlight's embrace, let your spirit ride.

Soliloquy of the Sunset Trellis

Oh, the vines are speaking, it's quite absurd,
Their whispers are giggles, it's truly unheard!
Flowers retell tales of the day gone by,
While sunbeams all chuckle, painting the sky.

A zany old owl thinks he's quite the sage,
Preening his feathers, a true feathered mage.
Crickets are crooning a comedic serenade,
Their legs all a-clicking, no notes gone to fade.

The dusk wears a grin, as colors collide,
As orange turns purple, the shadows abide.
Worms wiggle and wiggle, in a mischief spree,
What wisdom they share, just for you and me!

So let's toast to dusk, with a chuckle or two,
A raucous farewell, to the day that we blew!
In the twilight's embrace, may our giggles entwine,
For tomorrow awaits, with its own punchline.

Choir of the Canopied Twilight

High up in the branches, a whimsical choir,
Sing songs of the forest, with laughter afire!
The owls hum a melody, slightly off-key,
While the crickets provide their own symphony.

The trees clap their hands, as the fireflies dance,
A sparkly ballet, in a nightly romance.
With a wink and a nod, the stars join the tune,
Each glimmer a giggle, as bright as the moon.

Squirrels shake maracas, with zeal and delight,
Bouncing to rhythms, beneath the moonlight.
The breezes join in, with a tickle and tease,
Igniting a ruckus, swaying the leaves.

So gather your friends, let the party unfold,
In this joyful cacophony, let stories be told!
With harmony shared in laughter's sweet flight,
This woodland ensemble makes the heart feel light.

Whistles of the Wandering Winds

Hush now, can you hear what the breezes say?
With a playful whistle, they're off for the day!
Twirling through trees, they stumble and sway,
    Chasing each other, in a merry ballet.

Laughter erupts as they tickle the grass,
Spinning the daisies, they wiggle and pass.
They ruffle the leaves, causing quite the fuss,
    Even the insects erupt into rush!

"Hey look at that cloud!" says a wind with a grin,
    "Let's give it a hug, let the laughter begin!"
They dance round the meadows, with no signs of care,
    Turning the world into a carnival fair.

So, come take a stroll where the breezes will play,
    Join in their fun, let your worries decay!
For in every whistle, in each swirling bend,
    There's joy in the chaos, and laughter to lend.

Interlude of the Illuminated Thicket

In a thicket alive with chatter,
Squirrels dangle, chasing each other.
A frog sings loudly, a croaky tune,
While the birds join in, a feathery swoon.

Amidst the rustle, a misfit crow,
Struts and stumbles, says, 'Look at me go!'
He trips on a branch, what a sight to see,
The trees are laughing, as happy as can be.

A hedgehog joins in, steals the show,
With his quills poking fun, 'What do you know?'
The dance of the leaves in the warm breeze,
Makes critters chuckle with utter ease.

As the sun sets, they gather around,
To share silly tales where laughter is found.
In this woodland revelry, joy takes flight,
A quirky interlude, a magical night.

Harmonizing Hues Among the High Leaves

Up high, the colors tango and swirl,
As butterflies twirl in a playful whirl.
A chameleon giggles, 'Look at my skin!'
'Can you guess what color I'm wearing within?'

The vines twist and shout, like a leafy brigade,
While a raccoon conducts with a stick, unafraid.
The owl hoots in rhythm, a wise old beat,
As the sunlight winks, oh, isn't this sweet?

Frisky flowers dance, beads of dew in flight,
Spinning like tops in the warm daylight.
They laugh at the antics of ants on parade,
A grand performance, in the shade they've made.

With each leaf that flutters, laughter does rise,
In this colorful chorus, joy fills the skies.
The harmony sings through the bright, leafy maze,
In this vibrant world, we bask in the praise.

Nature's Choral Constellation

Beneath a sky of fluttering wings,
Frogs croak their jokes as the firefly sings.
An orchestra sways in a concert of light,
As critters convene for their late-night rite.

A squirrel on stage takes a deep, silly bow,
Crowd goes wild, 'How'd you do that?! Wow!'
While crickets click-click in synchronized glee,
The grasshoppers hop, adding melody.

With each rustling leaf, the laughter grows loud,
As a possum sings solo, feeling quite proud.
The trees tap their roots in the harmony,
A nature's concert, pure jubilee!

As stars peek out, their twinkle aligns,
With the joy of the forest, all worries decline.
In this celestial gathering, let's raise a toast,
To nature's own show, we love the most!

Twilight Reverberations

The sun bows low, the fun's just begun,
As dusk creeps in with a shimmering run.
A raccoon reveals his talents at night,
While owls give him notes in sheer delight.

Mice tap dance, wearing shoes made of grass,
While shadows play games, giving off sass.
The dragonflies zoom and swoosh all around,
In this glowing hour, hilarity's found.

Branches sway gently like they know a jest,
While the fireflies twinkle, all dressed in their best.
A clumsy beetle rolls by, puffing with pride,
The night air is filled with each chuckle and glide.

With laughter that echoes through twilight so bright,
Creatures unite in this magical night.
As stars wink down, they all take a pause,
In this playful orchestra, applause, applause!

Breeze Through the Branches

In the treetops, squirrels debate,
Who can swing? Who's really great?
A nut flies by, a daring toss,
They feign a gasp, but hold the gloss.

A jaybird sings a silly tune,
While leaves dance round, they're in a swoon.
The wind just giggles, quick and sly,
As acorns tumble from the sky.

A hanging cat made out of yarn,
Prowls the boughs like a leaf-born barn.
With every leap, he takes a shot,
Of laughter from the birds, a lot!

Oh, nature's park—such joy, such play,
In every branch, a bright ballet.
The canopy's a stage so grand,
For jesters clad in leaf and strand.

Flutters and Fables of the Foliage

A butterfly with polka dots,
Looks for treasures in hidden spots.
He opens books, page by page,
Of flower tales and garden sage.

A bumblebee, quite round and loud,
Buzzes rhymes, it sings out proud.
The petals blush with every sound,
In fragrant tales that swirl around.

Grasshoppers joke about their age,
While spiders weave a tangled stage.
With every hop, a giggle shared,
A tapestry of fun declared.

In this green realm, fables soar,
With laughter echoing evermore.
The leaves listen, they rustle near,
To every tale, to every cheer.

Whirl of Whimsical Whispers

Up in the limbs, the whispers twirl,
A secret gang of leaves that whirl.
They plot and plan, so sly and neat,
For pranks on squirrels, oh what a feat!

The raccoons roll with laughter bold,
As tree frogs croak the tales of old.
Each breeze a chuckle, soft and bright,
As shadows dance—a quirky sight.

The dappled sun plays peekaboo,
With every giggle, it slips on through.
And if you listen, soft and clear,
You'll hear the banter, do lend an ear!

In this raucous, leafy caper,
Nature jests—there's no better paper.
The whispers hee-haw, the wind will sigh,
As mischief reigns beneath the sky.

Sanguine Serenades of the Subtle

In dusky light, the shadows tease,
A gopher laughs, takes life with ease.
With every swoop, the willows sway,
As fireflies join the evening play.

A raccoon strums a twiggy lute,
While crickets keep a steady root.
The leaves applaud with rustling cheer,
For every joke that's sung so clear.

A chorus of frogs croaks tunes so sweet,
While the moon dips low to join the beat.
The stars giggle, blink in delight,
To serenades that last till night.

In this enchanting natural show,
Each rustle, each giggle makes spirits glow.
So come and revel in whimsy's flow,
Where nature's humor steals the show.

Hymn of the Heartwood

In the grove where squirrels play,
Chasing acorns day by day.
Poised on branches, quite a sight,
Chattering birds take to flight.

Frogs in suits, they croak and leap,
Hiding treasures, secrets keep.
Rabbits laughing at the wind,
Whiskers twitching, mischief pinned.

Twirling vines with clever flair,
Swinging round without a care.
Laughter echoes, leaves all sway,
Nature's jesters in a play.

Whimsical, the trees all hum,
As the buzzing bees go numb.
Joyful chaos in the glade,
Every creature, unafraid.

Echoes in theairy Vault

Whirly wings, the flies do spin,
Tickling noses on a whim.
Mice in sneakers, feeling spry,
Wobbling past, oh my, oh my!

Clouds of laughter, trees that grin,
A bustling world where jokes begin.
Each branch holds a hidden jest,
Nature's comedy at its best.

Raccoons in hats, a funny sight,
Playing pranks by morning light.
Every nook seems to conspire,
With giggles that never tire.

Bouncing bunnies join the fun,
Dancing 'neath the warming sun.
Together, they weave a tale,
Of whimsy spun on leafy trail.

Fragments of Forest Phantoms

Ghosts of trees with funny bones,
Whispering secrets in funny tones.
Rustling leaves, a dance so spry,
Shadows laughing as they fly.

Mushrooms giggle in a row,
Sprouting tales of joy to grow.
Elves in boots, oh what a crew,
Stomping puddles, splashes too.

Pixies chuckle, twirling near,
Each little blink a burst of cheer.
In the twilight, whimsy's here,
Celebrating with cheer and beer.

Songs of crickets make us smirk,
Add to this the frogs that lurk.
Nature's pranksters, always wry,
In this realm where laughter's high.

Murmurings of the Moonlit Wood

Moonbeams tap-dance on the leaves,
Nonsense giggles in the eaves.
Owls play cards, wise with a wink,
Trees lean closer, hear them think.

A raccoon chef stirs a stew,
In a pot of vines and dew.
Fireflies buzzing, lighting up,
As the night spills from the cup.

Frogs in tuxedos take a stand,
Hosting parties, oh so grand!
Dancing shadows skip around,
In the dark, joy can be found.

Moonlit whispers, soft and bright,
Every creature's pure delight.
Wandering through this merry wood,
Every giggle understood.

Echoing Silhouettes

Beneath a tree, the squirrels play,
Chasing shadows, come what may.
Acorns fall like drumbeats loud,
While birds gossip in their crowd.

A raccoon sneaks with stealthy grace,
Stealing snacks, it sets the pace.
With every scamper, giggles rise,
As branches wiggle, hide their spies.

Sunbeams dance on mottled ground,
A waltz of whispers all around.
Frogs croak tunes like off-key jesters,
While beetles march like tiny testers.

In leafy arms, the laughter swells,
Echoes bounce like playful bells.
The forest holds a vibrant cheer,
Where silly things bring joy, my dear.

Silenced by the Shadows

In the dusk, a shadow lurks,
Whistling tunes with funny quirks.
A turtle trips on leafy trails,
While crickets chirp in silly tales.

The moon peeks through like a sly eye,
As owls hoot, "Who?" and nearly cry.
A firefly's dance, a blinking show,
While chasing dreams, on moonbeams flow.

A fox pretends to take a snooze,
But giggles slip; the secret's loose.
Rabbits hop in comic fright,
As shadows dance and tease the night.

The night confides in whispers low,
Stifled laughs in the twilight glow.
Even silence plays the fool,
In this woodland, life's a school.

Whispers Beneath the Leaves

A chatty breeze through branches weaves,
Spinning tales of rustling leaves.
In critter meetings, secrets dwell,
As laughter bubbles, who can tell?

A chipmunk with a nutty grin,
Proclaims to all, "Let's begin!"
With twists and turns, the stories flow,
As fireflies join the sparkling show.

Squirrels somersault from high above,
With acrobatic flips, they shove.
The laughing brook, a chatterbox,
Mixes in with wise old ducks.

In every nook, a giggle hides,
While frogs perform in silly strides.
Beneath the leaves, joy takes its stand,
Echoing laughter across the land.

Symphony of the Forest Floor

Where tree roots twist like notes in song,
The forest floor plays all day long.
With mushrooms tapping little feet,
Each sound a quirky, wild treat.

Ants march in line, a tiny band,
Carrying crumbs, so carefully planned.
The toadstools nod, they join in tune,
While gophers groove beneath the moon.

Branches creak in rhythmic sway,
Chirping crickets join the fray.
A raccoon croons a silly tune,
Beneath the watchful eye of the moon.

With laughter ringing clear and bright,
The forest hums into the night.
A symphony of joyous cheer,
Is played by all who wander near.

Chords from Above

Amidst the leaves, the birds take flight,
Their tweets and chirps, a pure delight.
Squirrels chime in, the nuts in tow,
A musical prank, oh what a show!

A raccoon strums on an old guitar,
While crickets croon from near and far.
With every note, they dance and sway,
A silly concert, brightening the day!

Branches sway to the balmy breeze,
Nature's rhythm puts minds at ease.
Yet who knew that a frog could sing,
A jolly tune, fit for a king!

So join the tune, oh let it fly,
In this leafy realm, let laughter cry.
For in the woods, the humor thrives,
In chords from above, the joy arrives.

Harmonies of Height

Up high in the trees, the laughter spills,
As monkeys play tag, climbing hills.
A chorus of giggles fills the air,
With antics so wild, you can't help but stare.

Parrots perform in colorful coats,
While a wise old owl just chuckles and gloats.
Frogs leap in tune, hopping along,
Creating a jig, in nature's own song.

Breezes carry the jokes on their wings,
As squirrels play pranks like silly kings.
The sun sets low, painting skies bright,
In the harmonies of height, laughter takes flight.

So grab a seat on a branch so wide,
Join the woodland crowd, let humor be your guide.
In this playful realm, let's stay awhile,
Where nature's orchestra always brings a smile!

Notes Beneath the Boughs

Under the boughs where shadows play,
A turtle spins tales that make day sway.
With each gentle breeze, a tickled laugh,
As rabbits join in, crafting a half.

The leaves rustle softly, whisper sweet,
While busy bees dance on tiny feet.
A song from a brook, with splashes galore,
And all of a sudden, the jester's in store!

Chipmunks beatbox in rapid delight,
Hitching a ride on a leaf's flag flight.
Who knew that the forest could giggle and tease?
In notes beneath boughs, we find joy with ease.

So step to the rhythm of nature's craze,
And join in the fun, let your heart blaze.
With melodies sweet, beneath lofty trees,
Life in the woods is a whimsical tease!

Serenade of the Sunlit Grove

In the sunlit grove, where shadows dance,
A hedgehog spins tales of romance.
With a flick of his paws, he steals the show,
While crickets hum softly, a concert in tow.

A family of owls sway side to side,
With glasses perched on beaks, oh what a ride!
The sun drips gold as laughter ignites,
In this serenade, everything delights.

Breezy whispers play tag with the sun,
As nature's own band has just begun.
Frogs craft their beats, while rabbits leap high,
In a merry-go-round, under a sky.

So gather round for a whimsical cheer,
The grove tells a tale that's truly dear.
In adventures of laughter, we'll forever roam,
In the serenade of the sunlit grove, we feel at home!

Whirlwind of Whispers

In a forest full of chatter,
Where squirrels chatter all the time,
The bushes wave like giggling kids,
With acorns rolling in a rhyme.

The leaves are knocking, what a show!
Mice are dancing on their toes,
The wind plays tags with branches high,
As nature puts on quite a pose.

The flowers snicker in the breeze,
While shadows shimmer, twist, and shout,
A pelican trips, a frog just grins,
Their silly antics never pout.

Just listen close to all the fun,
Nature's symphony on the run,
With whispers bouncing everywhere,
It's quite a wild, whimsical pun!

Echoing Shadows of the Grove

In the woods, a sneaky tune,
Leaves hit jigs from noon to moon,
Owls wear hats, and fetch their drinks,
While robins plot and giggle, winks.

Beneath the branches, shadows dart,
Frogs and crickets play their part,
A chorus of snorts and squeaks,
As nature giggles, never weak.

A moose slips by with quite a flair,
Swaying low, he's unaware,
The bushes weep with laughter loud,
The trees cheer on; they're feeling proud.

When shadows rise and laughter grows,
The forest plays its silly shows,
With echoes bouncing through the trees,
It's pure delight, a joy that frees!

Swaying Shadows

Underneath a wobbly tree,
The shadows giggle with great glee,
A raccoon prances with a crown,
While chipmunks bounce up and down.

The breeze is tickling all around,
Pine needles dance upon the ground,
Their rustling rhythm interrupts,
As birds make silly little clucks.

Crickets chirp a merry song,
While creatures play all night long,
A fox tripped over roots he found,
Echoes laughed; he spun around!

In this dream of leafy play,
Laughter fills the night and day,
With swaying shadows, fun unfolds,
Nature's jest, a tale retold!

Soaring Sounds

High above in azure skies,
A parrot cracks the funniest lies,
While eagles swoop with goofy grace,
Their flying tricks, a silly race.

A chorus of beeps and caws,
Echo through the forest jaws,
With owls that hoot in funny tones,
They shake their feathers, tickle bones.

The wind's a playful, cheeky friend,
It sends the whispers without end,
A turtle grins, a beetle rolls,
Together joining in their roles.

Above it all, the sounds combine,
Creating laughter, pure divine,
As soaring sounds fill up the air,
In nature's circus, we all share!

Crescendo of Chirping Life

With dawn's first light, the chorus starts,
A symphony of furry hearts,
Chirps and croaks, a tuneful brawl,
A melody that echoes all.

Sparrows sing of breakfast treats,
A raccoon stumbles on its feet,
The crickets wink and croon along,
In this funny, chirping throng.

The bumblebees join in the beat,
Buzzing round, they quicken their feet,
While ladybugs play a silly game,
Swaying 'round like they're in a frame.

In crescendo, life takes its flight,
From day to day, with pure delight,
A joyful ruckus, here to stay,
In nature's laughter, we all play!

www.ingramcontent.com/pod-product-compliance
Lightning Source LLC
Chambersburg PA
CBHW051646160426
43209CB00004B/805